Raising the Perfect Puppy

A Guide to Housebreaking, Crate Training & Basic Dog Obedience

SHANNON O'BOURNE & PETER WHITMAN

"Raising the Perfect Puppy" by Shannon O'Bourne and Peter Whitman. Published by Walnut Publishing Company, Hanover Park, IL 60133

www.walnutpub.com

FREE BOOK CLUB INVITE

Before we get started with our puppy training book, we wanted to invite you, our valued Walnut Publishing reader, to join our Free Book Club.

Claim your invitation at **www.walnutpub.com** to get notified when we have new releases, discounts and more books about dogs from our small press.

Thanks for buying, and enjoy reading.

CONTENTS

Introduction i

1 Puppy Training Basics 1

2 Setting Ground Rules & Routine 6

3 Positive Reinforcement 10

4 Reading Puppy Body Language 15

5 10 Potty Training Commandments 20

6 Puppy Crate Training 26

7 Teaching 'Sit' 30

8 Teaching 'Down' 33

9 Teaching 'Stay' 36

10 Teaching 'Come' 39

11 Teaching 'Heel' 42

Conclusion 45

Further Reading 46

INTRODUCTION

Thank you for buying "Raising the Perfect Puppy." You are taking the first step of a responsible puppy parent, to learn how to give your puppy every chance to be successful in life as he or she grows into a lovable, good dog.

We hope to guide you on your way to becoming a pet parent that your puppy admires, respects, and trusts.

Puppy training is all about building a solid foundation of communication and respect between you and your dog. In this book, you'll learn everything you need to know to prepare to puppy train, how to use positive reinforcement to build trust with your puppy, and finally, how to potty train, crate train, and teach five essential dog obedience commands.

Once again, thanks for purchasing, and please let us know if there's anything we can help you with. We're just an email away at contact@walnutpub.com

Enjoy!

CHAPTER 1
PUPPY TRAINING BASICS

"Happiness is a warm puppy."

—Charles M. Schulz

As a new puppy parent, you're probably excited, nervous, and hopeful that your little pup will grow into a well-behaved dog and loyal companion. There is so much to learn about your new pup, so let's not waste any time and get straight to the important stuff. Good luck!

PUPPY TRAINING BEGINS IMMEDIATELY

Once you get your little guy (or gal) home, training should start immediately. Don't waste time fretting over the perfect toys, dog bed, collar color or name. (OK, do pick a good name!) The most important thing that determines the success of your puppy in his early life and turning into a well-behaved dog "teenager" and adult is your relationship with him from day one.

Puppies learn very quickly, and if you don't start reinforcing good behavior and appropriate behavior from the start, your puppy will start picking up bad habits immediately, and it will be harder to correct these down than the line than if you just start off on the right foot.

You should be prepared to feel a lot of emotions throughout the first few weeks and months of owning a puppy. It's not easy, believe us, we have years of puppy training experience. There come many frustrations, annoyances, struggles and more. Owning a puppy and raising it to behave well is not a walk in the park.

However, if you follow the tips, guides and steps for training that you will find in this book, your puppy will have the advantages he or she needs to live a successful, full, happy and obedient doggy life.

So, prepare yourself to feel some sadness or frustrations. Be prepared to question your own competence when trying to train. But know that these emotions are also normal responses to puppy ownership. The best thing to do is not get mad at yourself, to be patient with your puppy as well as yourself, and to remain calm, cool and collected.

Dogs are very sensitive to small body language changes, and they will be able to tell when you are sad. This means they might cheer you up with some extra snuggles when you're feeling down, but it also means if you're feeling frustrated, stressed or unconfident, your dog will feel the same.

So project confidence, authority and calm to your puppy, and you will find your puppy mirroring back these positive emotions.

WHY IS TRAINING SO IMPORTANT?

Training is of the upmost importance because it is the way you and your pup learn to communicate with each other, and it establishes the groundwork for the relationship you will have throughout your puppy's entire adult dog life. **Training is communication.**

If you start building a relationship based on trust, communication, clear expectations, and leading your puppy toward the success of being obedient and gaining new skills, you both will benefit. You will both be happier and feel closer to each other. **Training builds trust.**

Learning to obey your commands, how to navigate his or her new home, and interact with you is a lot for a new puppy. It is also a lot for a human! Communication is hard in human relationships sometimes, and we have all the advantages of a shared language. So it is more difficult in-between species, especially when one of those partners is but a baby!

So again, remember to bring patience and calm to your training sessions.

TRAINING A PUPPY IS LIKE RAISING A CHILD

Training is additionally crucial for your puppy because it is showing them the boundaries of their world. Puppies and dogs want to understand the world they live in, just like humans. You know to drive on the right side of the street, to leave a tip at restaurants, and how to greet people. Some basic things, like saying "hello," "goodbye," "please" and "thank you" were taught by your parents when you were young. They taught you good manners, just like you will teach your puppy good manners.

Some things you learned as you grew older. You learned about driving in driver's education, and how to tip from social norms and maybe from your friends. You can feel how difficult it is to travel to a different country where the cultural customs, methods of greeting, and maybe even side of the street cars drive on is different. You feel out of place, like you can't understand, and like you may be behaving improperly.

But just like training a puppy, if you have a guide who tells you the customs of the new culture, you can make your way. This is what you are teaching your puppy: You are teaching him or her the customs of the human world, the expectations of the dog-human relationship, and what is expected of them.

Just like raising a child, your puppy will test boundaries and push back on some things. This is normal. Just move ahead with your training and reinforce what you are teaching. Your dog will live a healthier, happier life because of it.

CONSISTENCY AND ROUTINE ARE KEY

As you go through our book about puppy training, you may wonder how often to do the training recommended in here. The most important thing for your new puppy is **consistency and routine.**

For example, during potty training, when your puppy eliminates in the back yard, the action needs to be met with a reward every time. When your puppy is chewing, it needs to be met with a "no" every time. Every action must have a predictable and consistent reaction. Otherwise your puppy will get confused, and training will proceed much slower.

Routine is also key. In the beginning of potty training, for example, you should take your puppy outside to eliminate every hour. Your puppy should be fed at the same times every day. This routine helps give the puppy a sense of normalcy. They are in a new environment, with a new caretaker, and there is a lot of new stimulation.

But, at the same time, puppies have very short attention spans. This means you will need to keep training session as short as possible. Do not train for long periods, but take breaks to let your puppy be a puppy and have fun and roll around on the floor with you. Training should be fun!

CLICKER TRAINING AND REWARDS

Before you begin puppy training, you should be familiar with clicker training. Clicker training is widely considered the most precise and effective method of dog training in the industry, and purchasing a clicker (usually less than $2 online or in a pet store) is definitely worth the investment.

So how does clicker training work? When your puppy performs an action correctly, you use the plastic clicker to make a loud "CLICK" sound. Then immediately after, you give your puppy a treat reward. The point is that your puppy begins to associate the click with a treat reward, and he or she knows that the click means a behavior has been performed precisely and correctly.

If you only use treat rewards, sometimes you may fumble with getting treats from your pocket, or you don't say the command exactly when you should, and your puppy is confused about what behavior exactly is being rewarded. With the click, you can precisely and accurately communicate to your puppy what action earned the reward.

Always make sure to click before giving the treat reward, as you want your puppy to solely associate the click with doing well, and not another action, for example, if you are reaching for food *at the same* time as making the click.

What sort of treats make good rewards? It is best to use small, bite size treats, as you will be using them often to reinforce good behavior. You can pick up puppy or dog treats from your local pet store, but remember that your little puppy will get full a lot faster than a full grown Great Dane!

You can also use human food to reward your dog, like carrots, apple pieces, sardines, non-butter air-popped popcorn, or veggies. **Do not feed foods that are harmful to dogs**, like chocolate, grapes, avocado, or raisins. Always double-check with a search online before feeding a food to your puppy, and avoid a trip to the emergency room. Many human foods are even lethal to dogs, so always check.

That is a basic introduction to puppy training, are you getting excited to grow and build your special relationship with your new best friend? We hope so.

In the next chapter, we'll discuss your puppy's daily routine and how to set some ground rules for behavior.

KEY TAKEAWAYS FROM CHAPTER 1

- A well-trained puppy needs boundaries and to understand his place in the world and your home

- The most important thing for training your new puppy is consistency and routine

- Raising a puppy can be like raising a kid: They will test their boundaries

- Be patient. It is normal to frustrated when training a new puppy

- Clicker training is the most precise way to train your puppy

- Use dog-safe, healthy, small treats to reward your puppy for good behavior

CHAPTER 2
SETTING GROUND RULES AND ROUTINE

"Training a puppy is like raising a child. Every single interaction is a training opportunity."

—Ian Dunbar

Like we said in the last chapter, consistency and routine are key to setting up your puppy for a life of obedience, good behavior, and success. Wildly varying responses to behavior or changes in routine will only delay, hamper and maybe even prevent your puppy from learning all he needs to, to become a functioning member of your household.

In this chapter, we will look at just what you need to do to help your puppy feel safe in his or her routine.

CONSISTENCY IN ENVIRONMENT

When you bring your new puppy home, he should have all his things set up for him in the places they will go. You can introduce him to where his food and water bowls will be kept, where his bed will be, where his toys are kept, etc.

In terms of your puppy's bed, it is important that it is in a space in which he is entirely safe and protected. It should be an area of the home without high traffic, and preferably, his bed is in a corner of the room, so he feels walled off and safe from surprises. You can also use a crate, as we will discuss in Chapter 6 on crate training.

No one else should spend time in his bed; no cuddling from humans or other pets sneaking in for a quick nap. Dogs like to have one area that is completely their own, like a "den," and your puppy will feel safer with his very own bed. You can also put a ticking clock near his bed, as this may be like the sound of the heartbeat of his mom or littermates. This may help him feel safe and relaxed.

For food and water, this should go in an area with hardwood or tile, as some puppies and dogs are messy eaters. It should not be in the middle of a room, as this is stressful for a dog. Place the food and water bowls against a wall in a room of your home. Many people prefer the kitchen.

One note about puppies and food is that you do not want your puppy to grow into a food-aggressive dog. This is a dog that is possessive of his food and becomes nervous anytime someone is nearby. As children often have poor boundaries with dogs, an unwitting child could upset a food-aggressive dog and be injured by wandering near a dog when he is eating a snack.

To stop your puppy from becoming food possessive, you should distract him and touch him while he is eating. Roll a ball near him when he is eating, walk by him, pet him, move toward him quickly while he is eating. If your puppy does not respond to these stimuli and remains calm, click and reward with a treat. If your puppy growls or glares at you, do not reward the behavior. Just back off and try to train again at the next meal time.

Another environmental consistency aspect is time. Feed your puppy at the same time every day. Try to have a consistent wake-up and sleep routine for yourself, so he can predict when you will be awake and asleep and follow your schedule.

Remember, a puppy will be a hugely disruptive factor in the normalcy of your life, but the puppy should fit into your life; not the other way around.

EVERYONE ON THE SAME PAGE

Another important aspect of consistency and ground rules for your puppy is making sure that everyone in the household treats him or her the same, and applies the same corrective behaviors and encouragements.

If everyone treats your puppy differently, he will automatically defer to the person who lets him get away with the most bad behavior. Everyone should be on the same page in terms of puppy training, and even if there will be one primary trainer, everyone else needs to reinforce and not detract from what the puppy is learning.

Decide before the puppy arrives home what he is allowed to do and what he is not allowed to do. Can he go on any furniture? Are certain rooms off limits? Can he play-wrestle with the kids, or is this not allowed? Decide this beforehand so your puppy is not confused. It is harder to un-learn a behavior once he has been allowed to do it in an environment. If the rules are the same from the get-go, he has a much better chance of learning good puppy behavior in your home.

Choose commands that everyone can use with the puppy, even if everyone is not using a clicker for training. Some simple ones are a swift, sharp, loud "No," for bad behavior, and "Yes" or "Good" for good behavior. Just keep them consistent.

In the next chapter, we will discuss the training philosophy of positive reinforcement, in which you will learn to gain the trust of your puppy.

KEY TAKEAWAYS FROM CHAPTER 2

- Everyone in the home needs to be on the same page with training the puppy

- Some simple commands to use and implement across all family members are "no" and "good"

- Give your puppy a safe space he can call his own for his bed. You can also use a crate

- Put your puppy's food and water bowls in one place

- Distract your puppy while eating and reward for calm behavior so he does not become food-aggressive

- Try to keep a regular routine for your puppy for his eating schedule, and wake/sleep cycle

CHAPTER 3
POSITIVE REINFORCEMENT

"Whoever said you can't buy happiness forgot little puppies."

—Gene Hill

You are your puppy's protector. You are his parent, his friend, his guardian. His teacher, his mentor, and his playmate. You are his caretaker, his role model, and his best friend.

A relationship with a dog is unlike any other between man and animal. You have a huge responsibility on your hands, and if you contribute to your dog's life, you will find he can contribute to your life and enrich it in profound ways.

But like any relationship, whether between human and human or animal and human, it needs to be based on trust and built on communication. Puppy training is Communication 101 for your furry friend, and will establish how your relationship will go for the next 12 to 15 years of your dog's life.

If you take this responsibility seriously, and use the tactics outlined in this book, you will be rewarded with a loving, trusting, beautiful relationship. In this chapter, you will learn about positive reinforcement, the guiding philosophy of our puppy training.

WHAT IS POSITIVE REINFORCEMENT?

Positive reinforcement is a training philosophy that relies on positive rewards to reinforce behavior.

What this means is that when your puppy does something good, like sitting on command or eliminating outside, you reward him with something important to him, that he desires.

Puppies have simple needs. They like food, praise, petting, and spending time with their human. They love playtime, and frequent naps. The easiest and one of the most rewarding items for a puppy or any dog is a food treat. So for training your puppy, we recommend always reinforcing behavior with a special food treat.

Only use a treat that is safe for dogs. Many "human" foods like chocolate, grapes, raisins, avocado and more are dangerous and even lethal for canines. Google any human food before feeding to your puppy. You can use small bits of apple, carrot, or dog treats you buy from your local pet shop. Don't be shy about also sprinkling in praise and pets in addition to food treats when rewarding for good behavior.

In positive reinforcement training, it is best to use a clicker, outlined in Chapter 1. Whenever your puppy performs a good behavior, click and reward with a treat.

WHAT IS NEGATIVE REINFORCEMENT, OR PUNISHMENT?

There are two more methods of animal behavior training in addition to positive reinforcement.

Punishment is adding a stimulus your dog doesn't like to deter him from bad behavior. Negative reinforcement is removing a stimulus your dog doesn't like to reward him. In both cases, you are doing something to your puppy that causes him discomfort, pain or distress.

Building a relationship with a puppy is even more delicate than building one with a dog. Whereas a dog with even just a few years of experience knows a lot about the world, a puppy is just learning about it. How you treat your puppy will impact him or her for the rest of their life. Just like children are more impressionable than adults, you need to be a safe and gentle guide and teacher for your puppy.

If you break trust with your puppy by using punishment or negative reinforcement in training, your puppy will fear you, and become skittish, nervous and maybe even agitated and aggressive. Even gentle thwacks or spanks are adding an element of physical force that can make your dog sensitive to someone touching his rear-end, or generally nervous about human interactions.

We recommend you stay 100% away from any sort of training that uses shock collars, prong collars, physical punishment, or anything resembling making your dog uncomfortable.

Go with your gut, and only do what makes you comfortable with your puppy, even if you come across dog trainers or puppy training materials that encourage punishment. At the end of the day, you are the one who is spending your life with your puppy, and you have to answer for your behavior choices.

We recommend only using positive reinforcement. If you do, you are laying, brick-by-brick, the foundation for a healthy, trusting and awesome relationship with your dog.

GOOD EMOTIONAL AND MENTAL HEALTH

Your puppy is totally reliant on you: For food, for a home, for safety, for guidance, understanding his world and his boundaries.

How can you help your puppy become a well-adjusted adult dog? As this chapter has discussed, the first piece of the puzzle is positive reinforcement.

The second piece of the puzzle is going slow with puppy training. All puppies learn at a different speed and have different abilities. Just like people, dogs will learn in different ways and excel in different areas. Becoming frustrated during training is normal, but remember to never, ever take it out on your puppy.

Above all else, give your puppy respect, and they will show you the same, at least they will in a few months, when they have developed more of their dog brain. For now, patience is key. A puppy is like a baby; they cannot reason or think as well as when they are older. A puppy is a vulnerable, immature animal and a good trainer is forgiving and kind. Mistakes will happen, but they cannot be punished. It is only fruitful to reward the good behaviors, and you will quickly see the other behaviors diminish.

If your puppy has come from a shelter, he will be used to a lot of sound and stimulation. Being in a home is a very different environment, and your puppy will also need some time to get used to it. Be patient and give him time, and be realistic with your training goals. Many puppy training books promise quick fixes and potty training success in just three days. By following the strategies in this book for training your puppy, success will come in time. Be wary of puppy trainers who guarantee success immediately.

GOOD PHYSICAL HEALTH

Positive reinforcement is another good way to set your puppy up for success as he goes through all the rituals of puppy life: grooming, vet check-ups, meeting new people. A lot of these situations can make a tiny puppy nervous, but if he has experience being touched and handled all over, these situations will not be as nerve-wracking for him.

So, to train your puppy to get used to many different situations and vet check-ups, make sure he is comfortable with being touched all over his body.

Go slowly, but touch him on his paws, tail, hindquarters, snout, chest and belly. Every time he doesn't react and remains calm, click and reward.

You do not want your puppy to grow up being sensitive to people touching his paws, for example. When he is a strong, larger dog, he will be much less forgiving to professionals who need to clip his nails.

There are many ways you can use positive reinforcement to help your pup grow into a self-assured, calm and friendly dog. In this book, you will only be using positive reinforcement, but you will find that it is an essential and effective training method. In the next chapter, we will discuss reading puppy body language to better communicate with your dog.

KEY TAKEAWAYS FROM CHAPTER 3

- Positive reinforcement is using a reward to show your puppy that he has performed a good behavior

- Punishment and negative reinforcement use distressing or uncomfortable stimuli to train your dog. These methods should be avoided, as they erode trust and beget a frightened, nervous dog

- Whenever your puppy performs a desired action, use the clicker to click and give a food reward and petting and praise

- Positive reinforcement is the key to a well-adjusted, happy, confident puppy that grows into a good dog

- Use positive reinforcement to prepare your puppy for vet exams and grooming

CHAPTER 4
READING PUPPY BODY LANGUAGE

"There is no psychiatrist in the world like a puppy licking your face."

—Bernard Williams

Puppy training is learning how to communicate in your special animal-human relationship. One of the most essential forms of communications, whether between humans or animals or both, is body language.

Reading puppy and dog body language is easy, once you know what to look for. Just like humans use our posture, hands, eyes, and more to communicate with our bodies, dogs too use their mouth, eyes, tail and posture to show how they ae feeling to others.

Let's dive in to learning about dog posture, and what to look for to understand better what your puppy is telling you.

AGGRESSIVE BODY LANGUAGE

It's important to be aware of what dog body postures and movements mean that a dog is feeling aggressive and has the potential to defend itself. Puppies are still learning what is appropriate, and attacking anyone is definitely not appropriate.

If your puppy is feeling aggressive, he will display a few tell-tale signs. The first way a dog shows his or her feelings when feeling threatened is to look physically bigger. A dog or puppy achieves looking bigger by puffing out their chest, standing tall, and perking up their ears and tail. They may raise the hair on the back of their neck or their back as well.

Another sign that a dog or puppy is feeling aggressive is the "whale eye." This means opening the eyes very wide, and in some cases, the dog will give you the "side-eye," or looking at something out of the corner of his eye, instead of turning his head. You will be able to see the whites of your dog's eyes.

Usually very stiff body posture accompanies the "whale eye," and sometimes low growling as well. Sometimes dogs will pull back their lips to bare their teeth. This lip movement is a sign of aggression, whether or not it is accompanied by growling.

Lastly, dogs are very sensitive to eye contact. Between dogs, a staring contest is a way to assert dominance. Lower-status dogs will look away first when a higher-status dog stares them down. Therefore, avoid staring directly into your dog's eyes for a long period of time. Obviously, eye contact will be natural, but long periods of staring should be avoided.

SUBMISSIVE BODY LANGUAGE

Just like dogs display aggressive or dominant body language, dogs (and your puppy) can also display submissive body language.

Just like the opposite of aggression, where a dog tries to make himself look bigger, with submission, a puppy will try to make himself look small when threatened. That means crouching low near the ground, or lowering his head. He may also get as low as possible and display his stomach, a very vulnerable position, but one that could also be innocuous and just mean your puppy wants belly rubs! When assessing dog body language and behavior, context must always be taken in to consideration. Are you playing with your puppy, or is there a loud sound that may be intimidating him? Pay attention to context to help read dog body language.

A wagging tail can mean a happy pup, as everyone knows, but it can also mean submission. If your puppy is displaying another sign of submission, a slow-wagging tail may mean your dog feels intimidated. A tail curled around your dog's bottom, or curled all the way between his legs, is a sure sign that a dog feels small and intimidated, maybe even afraid. The last sign of submission is half-closed eyes.

Be on the lookout for these signs of submission when training your pup. You want your pup to feel calm and confident during training, not intimidated and submissive. We will talk about how to make your puppy more comfortable with your own body language at the end of this chapter, but first, let's look at a fun body language section: The happy pup.

PLEASURE/HAPPINESS/NEUTRAL BODY LANGUAGE

A happy pup is one of the best things in the world, isn't it? A dog that is happy to see you, having fun playing, or clearly content makes the heart melt. Here are the body language signs your puppy will display when experiencing pleasure (or happiness), or just a neutral body posture.

Eyes half-closed were one sign of submission, but they can also be a sign of pleasure in a dog. An open mouth usually means a happy dog, and some say they can even see dogs "smiling." Of course, there is also the tail. Everyone knows that a wagging tail means a happy dog, and most of the time, this is absolutely true.

If your dog is alert and interested in something, he or she may have stiff body posture as they listen, smell, or try to gather more information about something. An alert body posture also includes a tail that is raised higher than 45 degrees from your dog's body.

You should see the following puppy body language a lot: If your puppy is ready to play, he will show you distinct signs that he is excited and playful. A puppy may raise down onto his front elbows, thereby leaving his butt in the air. This bowing down usually indicates a play mood. He may bark to get your attention, or raise one paw as well. He may chase after you, circling you, or bring a toy.

In this final chapter section, let's talk a little bit about how human body language appears to puppies.

YOUR BODY LANGUAGE

When training your puppy, your own body language is as important as being able to read your dog's. Canines are very sensitive to the human body and slight changes in composure. A dog will be able to pick up if you are feeling nervous, excited, tense, sad, or happy.

When training, it is best to be calm and confident. It is normal to feel frustrated sometimes, but take a break for your energy and to clear your head.

If you are training or interacting with your puppy and he displays aggressive behaviors, you want to give a firm "no" command, but not physically intimidate him by moving forward quickly or touching him. After one "no," let the situation diffuse and leave the room. Reward calm behavior at other times throughout the day.

If your puppy is submissive, you want to make him feel safe, as he is feeling nervous and intimidated and unsure. To make him feel safe, crouch down low, to get on his level. Open your arms. An aggressive posture is standing over your dog, as your height over his can be intimidating, especially for a small puppy. Staring is also aggressive, and should be avoided.

Now you should have a firm understanding of the puppy training basics, preparing for training, setting up a routine, using a clicker for positive reinforcement, and reading your puppy's body language.

In the next chapters of this book, you will learn some essential training for puppies. Most importantly, you will learn about housetraining your puppy. Crate-training will also be discussed. Let's get started on potty training!

KEY TAKEAWAYS FROM CHAPTER 4

- Understanding dog body language is the key to communicating with your puppy

- A puppy feeling aggressive will try to make himself appear bigger, may be stiff, and will give you the "whale eye"

- A puppy feeling submissive will try to make himself appear small and will have a curled tail

- A puppy ready to play will bow down, bark, run, or raise his paw

- A puppy that is alert may go stiff in the body and raise his tail and ears

- Your puppy will be able to read your body language, so be calm and confident during training

- If a puppy is feeling nervous, get on his level by crouching down and never stare

CHAPTER 5
PUPPY POTTY TRAINING
& THE TEN COMMANDMENTS

"A puppy is but a dog, plus high spirits, and minus common sense."

—Agnes Repplier

In the first four chapters of this book, you learned a lot about the right training method for your puppy. Hopefully you feel prepared as we move onto the most important behavior your puppy will learn in its life: Potty training.

This behavior means teaching your dog to eliminate outside only, and not inside on carpeting or rugs. It is a behavior that, if taught well, will last a lifetime.

Let's get to how to teach your puppy to be potty trained!

PREPARING TO POTTY TRAIN

The first thing to know about puppies and potty training is that puppies have small bladders, so they need to go more often than full-grown dogs, and also have less control over their bladder. Though this will mean many more trips outside during the first few months of owning your puppy, it's also great news because it means there are that many more opportunities to reinforce good potty training behaviors!

Without further ado, let's get to the 10 Commandments of Puppy Potty Training.

THE 10 COMMANDMENTS OF PUPPY POTTY TRAINING

1. ESTABLISH GOOD HABITS FROM THE START

For your puppy, learning how and when to eliminate will be difficult to grasp. This is something that has not been required of them before, and they will have to learn. Some may learn quickly; others slowly. The most important thing is to have a plan before you bring your puppy home, so you can be consistent from the very beginning.

Being in a new environment is like having a clean slate for the puppy, and he will learn more quickly if the rules at his new home are always consistent, instead of that he is allowed to potty inside for the first few days but then not after.

While some training materials promise guaranteed results in just a few days, remember that potty training is a not a race. It is about building a habit that is well-reinforced and long-lasting. Not having to re-teach potty training is more important than fast results that don't last.

2. KEEP YOUR PUPPY BY YOUR SIDE AT ALL TIMES

If you or someone else at home is able to keep the puppy with you at all times during potty training, you will be successful much faster. This is because you want to be able to see if your puppy begins showing signs that he needs to potty. Some of these signs are spinning in circles and sniffing the ground. If you constantly have your puppy with you, you will be able to learn what his patterns are before he has to go.

One way to make sure your puppy stays by your side is to keep him or her leashed at all times. It may be annoying, but it is the best way to keep them in your line of site at all times. Even if you are keeping the puppy in the same room with you, they could disappear for just a few seconds behind a chair to eliminate inside. If you get distracted for just a few seconds, it could mean another accident. So leashing may be the way to go.

3. TAKE YOUR PUPPY OUT EVERY HOUR

Consistency will be the name of the game for potty training. Give your pup the chance to potty outside every hour that you are awake. If you are finding frequent accidents are happening inside, cut it down to every 50 minutes, or 45 or 40. Also make sure to add in potty break chances about 15 to 20 minutes after your puppy eats a meal or gulps a whole bunch of water.

As you go about your day, you may forget when you need to take your puppy out. To make it easy, set an alarm on your phone to go off every hour to remind you. Potty breaks outside should be short. Give your puppy about 5 to 10 minutes to walk around. Just enough time for him to go if he needs to, but not enough time to get excited about playing outside.

4. OFFER TWO OVERNIGHT OPPORTUNITIES FOR POTTYING

Lucky for you, you don't have to set an alarm to get up every hour in the middle of the night to help your puppy learn to potty outside. But you should get up at least once or twice during the night to give your puppy the chance. As your dog grows older, he will gain more control over his bladder and be able to hold it throughout the night. For now, though, you are raising a baby dog, and human babies require assistance throughout the night, just like puppies.

You should also take your puppy out for a potty opportunity right before you go to bed and as soon as you wake up in the morning.

5. NO PLAY DURING POTTY BREAKS

Potty break opportunities should be short, around 5 minutes long, and have the goal of getting your puppy to eliminate. If he doesn't take the chance, that doesn't mean it's playtime outside or time to explore all the good smells in the backyard. It's "go, or no." So if your puppy is clearly not going to eliminate, cut the potty break opportunity short and go back inside. Refrain from playing with or praising your puppy for the next 10 minutes, so he does not associate going outside and coming back in as what he is being rewarded for.

It is most important that your puppy begin associating going outside with going potty. There is plenty of time for play later!

6. REPETITION AND CONSISTENCY ARE KEY

Remember that your puppy depends on you for his training. He can't just "get it" by himself, he needs your guidance. So stick to your hourly breaks as perfectly as possible, and pay close attention to what his behavior patterns are before he goes potty so you can recognize them in the future.

7.   ACCIDENTS HAPPEN; DON'T PUNISH THEM

Accidents are going to happen, no matter what. It is just a fact of owning a puppy and going through the potty training process. Don't get angry with your puppy; they cannot help themselves, and they are only learning. Do not punish your dog or even yell. Dogs cannot associate a past behavior with rewards or punishment; it must be immediate. So even if your dog went on the carpet less than a minute ago, he will learn nothing from any yelling or punishment you could give.

Instead, only focus on reinforcing his good behavior, when he does it right. The positive rewards will be enough. When an accident, happens, just quietly clean it up.

When your puppy has an accident, ask yourself what you did wrong; not what the puppy did wrong. How could you have prevented this? Were you watching him closely enough? Did you miss a potty break earlier in the day? Focus on where you can improve as a teacher; your puppy is depending on you.

8.   USE A CUE WORD

When you puppy successfully goes potty outside, say a cue word simultaneously to the puppy going to the bathroom, whether it is pee or poo. Some cue words you can use are "hurry up," "wee wee," or "toilet." Or you can make up your own. Say the cue word once as your dog begins going, and then once when he finished, and click and give the reward.

Eventually your puppy will associate your cue word with going to the bathroom, and you may be able to get him or her to go on command. If you can successfully train this, it will come in handy in the future when you have a busy schedule or are going on a long road trip.

9.   GIVE A REWARD FOR PROPER POTTYING, EVERY TIME

Rewarding your puppy for going potty is the most essential part of potty training. He needs to associate going to the bathroom outside with getting rewarded.

As discussed in Chapter 1, the best rewards are healthy, dog-safe and small treats. Using a clicker will give you even more precision over your training. So immediately after your puppy is done eliminating outside, use your cue word, click once to signify a job well done and give a small treat. You can also lavish on praise and petting, but make sure you use these methods in addition to a treat, and not in place of it.

The most important thing is rewarding the behavior, every time, immediately after it happens. Dogs cannot associate past events with rewards, so it needs to be immediate. Do not get distracted or play on your phone while taking your puppy on a potty break during potty training. Watch him constantly.

10. PATIENCE, PATIENCE, PATIENCE

The last commandment of puppy potty training is to have patience. Potty training a puppy can take a week or more. Slow reinforcement will build the habit with a solid foundation.

There you have it, the Ten Commandments of Puppy Potty Training. You should have a good idea of how to train your puppy to eliminate outside. Accidents will happen, but you are on your way to having a fully housetrained puppy, and that is the first major lesson of any puppy's life. Congrats!

In the last chapter, we will learn how to crate train a puppy, which may come in handy for potty training as well.

KEY TAKEAWAYS FROM CHAPTER 5

- Consistency is key for puppy potty training

- Take your puppy out every hour, and twice overnight

- Use a cue word to help your puppy associate it with going potty

- Never punish accidents

- Reward for a successful outdoor potty break, every time

- Do not allow potty breaks to turn into playtime

- Keep your puppy with you at all times so you can monitor his behavior and notice when he needs to go

CHAPTER 6
PUPPY CRATE TRAINING

"No symphony orchestra ever played music like a two-year-old girl laughing with a puppy."

—Bern Williams

In chapter 2, we talked about how important it is for your puppy to have a place of his own in the home. Dogs naturally want to have a "den" of their own, where they feel closed in and protected. For some owners, that means getting a crate for their puppy.

When a puppy has grown accustomed to his or her crate, and it is used responsibly and effectively, there are many benefits, such as easing separation anxiety, or a simple way of taking the puppy to the vet.

However, some people do abuse the crate by using it too much. We will address these concerns, and how to crate train your puppy, in this chapter.

HOW TO USE THE CRATE

We all know that puppies are prone to mischief, attracted to it like moths to a flame. A crate can be a great way to contain your puppy and know that they are not getting into dangerous household items, chewing on furniture, or getting into anything they shouldn't be.

The crate may also ease anxiety in your puppy. Dogs naturally protect areas, and when you are away from home, a puppy may feel overwhelmed trying to protect a huge area of a house or apartment. If the puppy is contained in its crate, it will feel comfortable only having to protect this small area.

How do you choose a crate? Get a crate that is big enough for your puppy to stand up and turn around in. It should be well-ventilated. It should be just big enough for bedding to fit in and cover all areas. This may help with potty training as well, as the puppy will not want to soil his bedding, so he will not want to go in his crate.

Overall, having a crate can help when behavior training your puppy.

HOW NOT TO USE THE CRATE

A puppy should not be left in its crate for hours at a time, generally more than 4. As discussed in the chapter on Potty Training, puppies have small bladders, and they do not want to soil their bedding, so having to go in the crate is very traumatic for them. Make sure to give them frequent potty breaks.

Your new puppy also probably wants to be with you as often as possible. Practicing putting your puppy in the crate is good while you are home, so he is more used to it while you are away, but it is not good to leave a puppy in the crate for 8 or 9 hours while you are at work. Having a puppy is a full-time job, and they need you when they are young. Make sure to have someone else you live with or a neighbor or professional dog walker let the puppy out several times throughout the day.

You should also not use the crate as punishment. You want your dog to enjoy being in it. It is his safe space, not a time-out area.

HOW TO CRATE TRAIN YOUR PUPPY

First of all, your puppy should feel comfortable in the crate, so put a bed that he loves in there, as well as water, and a few toys. Let him explore the crate on his own the first time you introduce him to it. If he doesn't want to go in on his own, first tie back the door to make sure it will not surprise the puppy by closing on him and scaring him.

The next step is to put some treats in the crate to encourage him to go inside. When he goes inside, use your clicker to reward this behavior and give him another treat and praise.

Some dogs are more nervous than others, and may not want to walk all the way inside at first. That is OK, let your puppy move at his own pace. Do a training session every day to encourage him to be able to walk in comfortably. Whatever you do, don't push your puppy into the crate. You never want him to associate something negative with the crate, as it should be a place he feels safe. If you even lightly push him into the crate, he will become nervous.

MEAL TIME IN THE CRATE

The next step in introducing your puppy to the crate is to feed his meals to him in the crate. If you puppy won't enter at first, just feed meals near the crate to start.

When the puppy is eating his meal comfortable in the crate, with his full body inside, you can close the door. It is best to have him facing you to close the door, so he can see what you are doing, and it does not come as a surprise. After each meal, have your puppy wait just a minute to be let out of the crate, to get used to being inside but not distracted by eating.

You should increase the time slowly over a period of days, until your puppy can be in the crate for 15 minutes. If the puppy begins whining, scratching or seems upset, you have lengthened the amount of time too quickly.

USING A CRATE COMMAND

When your dog is comfortable eating meals in the crate and being in it for short periods of time, the next step is to attach a command to the kennel. You can use "kennel" or "crate" or whatever you like. Use the same clicker system described in Chapter 1. When your puppy enters the crate, use your command, click, and give a treat reward. If you need to do it in steps, having your puppy just enter the threshold, then moving half in, then moving all the way in, go slowly and click-train for each of these steps.

Once your puppy can go in the crate on command, you can leave them in the crate for around 30 minutes while you are home, to test how they handle it. The next step is leaving when the puppy is in the crate. Use your command and click-reward to get your puppy in the crate, and then leave the house for a period of time. Don't make coming home an excitable occasion, make it calm and normal. Leave your puppy in the crate periodically while you are home so they don't think the create is only for when you are leaving them.

KEY TAKEAWAYS FROM CHAPTER 6

- Having a crate for your puppy helps him feel like he has his own place, his own "den" where he can be safe

- Do not leave your puppy in the crate for long periods of time or make it associated with punishment

- First get your puppy used to going in the crate on his own

- Begin feeding meals in the crate with the door closed

- Reward your puppy for going in the crate on your command

- You can leave your puppy in the crate several times throughout the day while you are home for short time periods

- Using a crate can keep your puppy safe and your home from being ruined by puppy mischief while you are not supervising

This has been a primer on training your puppy in crate training and potty training, and we hope you have found it helpful. Now you should have a good understanding of the basics of puppy training, why it is important to your relationship, how to clicker train your puppy, the basics of the training philosophy of positive reinforcement, and how to potty train and crate train your new little friend.

In the next section, we'll move onto training the five essential commands that every dog should know: sit, down, stay, come and heel.

CHAPTER 7
TEACHING 'SIT'

"No matter how little money and how few possessions you own, having a dog makes you rich."

—*Louis Sabin*

In In this chapter, we will learn how to teach your puppy 'sit,' widely considered the most essential dog command to know.

Having your puppy sit allows him to be calm, focused on you, and in a position that allows for many follow-up commands, like 'down,' or more fun ones like 'shake' or 'up.'

You can find those advanced commands in our companion book, but here we will focus on the five essential dog commands.

Are you ready? Let's teach your puppy to sit:

1. Prepare for the trick:
   a. Establish a good training environment (indoors, familiar, calm, free of distraction)
   b. Make sure your dog is a good mood for training (calm, attentive, not hyper or sleepy or hungry)
   c. Have your clicker and a pocket of healthy, small, bite-size and dog-safe treats at the ready
   d. Make sure your own energy and body language are calm, and you feel confident

2. Get your dog's attention with a click and treat reward
    a. He should be facing you
    b. This alerts him that a training session will begin
3. Take out a treat from your pocket so that your dog knows you have it
4. Start with the treat above your dog's nose, and move it slowly toward the back of his head, over his face. Your dog will follow the treat with his eyes and body, trying to keep it in his view, and his bottom should go down
5. As soon as his bottom hits the floor, say the command "sit"
6. Click your clicker immediately after saying "sit"
7. Immediately after clicking, reward with the treat
8. Release your dog from the sit by moving backward a step and having him come to you. Take out another treat if he does not immediately move from the sitting pose and this should encourage him. You can use the command "free" or none at all at this beginning stage.
9. Repeat steps 3 to 8 many times for up to 5 minutes and then take a break
10. Repeat with another training session if your dog is still interested and doing well with the 'sit' training session
11. When your dog has mastered this training technique, the next step is moving your empty hand over your dog's head, instead of using a treat. Keep reinforcing the 'sit' verbal command and clicking and rewarding with a treat.
12. The next step is saying the 'sit' command without moving a treat or your empty hand over your dog's head. Reward with a click and treat
13. When your dog has mastered the 'sit' command, begin training in other environments, so your dog does not think he only needs to obey the 'sit' command in one room. Slowly move to more challenging environments, leaving outdoors for last.
14. It can take weeks for a dog to master sit, so be patient.
15. Stop each training session before you lose your dog's attention. He should go into each training session excited, not worn out from the one that came before. You do not want your dog to start associating training with something boring or painful.

EXTRA TIPS FOR TRAINING 'SIT'

- You may need to put your dog on a leash if he is especially energetic

- If your dog is turning his body to keep the treat in his view, instead of sitting, do the training in a corner, so your dog cannot back up or turn as easily

- If your dog needs some assistance understanding that you want him to sit as the treat moves over his head, you can use your other hand to gently press on his bottom as a "hint." Do NOT push hard, as this can hurt your dog, make him nervous and therefore a less effective learner, and start to erode the trust in your relationship

- As you move the treat over your dog's head, do not raise it too high, as he may stay standing. Just over the head should work for him to sit.

- Instead of teaching 'sit' from the standing position to the down position, you can teach sit from the down position as well. In this method, your dog needs to be laying down to start. You then raise the treat so that his head raises, but not his back legs. This method can be trickier than the one we have used in the numbered steps, but may be preferable if your dog likes to lay down!

- Always remember patience, patience, patience is key! If your dog is not getting it, give him a break and start again tomorrow.

- Be aware of where you are asking your dog to sit. On a carpet is preferable, some dogs do not like to sit on cold tiles or hardwood, as it is cold on their bottom and a bit slippery. Make sure your dog has good traction.

- Use praise and petting intermittently as well as treats to reward your dog and build your relationship, especially as the final reward at the end of a session.

- Do not overuse the command 'sit.' If your dog is not complying, repeating 'sit' over and over will not only not help him understand what you want, but will devalue the word moving forward so that it means nothing to him.

Those are the steps for learning 'sit' with your puppy! Remember that consistent but short training is key, and in no time, your puppy will have mastered the good behavior of knowing the 'sit' command.

In the next chapter, we will look at learning the 'down' command.

CHAPTER 8
TEACHING 'DOWN'

"Life is a series of dogs."

—George Carlin

In this chapter, we will learn how to train your puppy the 'down' command, which refers to the position of lying down.

To teach your puppy this trick, it is best that he has already mastered the 'sit' position and can do it on command every time and with ease. He will need to be in this position to effectively learn the next step of 'down.'

The first few beginning steps of this trick are also the same for the 'sit' command, as you must prepare your environment.

Let's learn how to teach your puppy 'down'!

1. Prepare for the trick:
    a. Establish a good training environment (indoors, familiar, calm, free of distraction)
    b. Make sure your dog is a good mood for training (calm, attentive, not hyper or sleepy or hungry)
    c. Have your clicker and a pocket of healthy, small, bite-size and dog-safe treats at the ready
    d. Make sure your own energy and body language are calm, and you feel confident
2. Get your dog's attention with a click and treat reward
    a. He should be facing you

b.   This alerts him that a training session will begin

3. Take out a treat from your pocket so that your dog knows you have it
4. Get your dog into the sitting position with the 'sit' command
5. Squat in front of him so that you are on his level
6. Move the treat downward from in front of his face so that he follows it with his head and lays down
7. Say the 'down' command as he moves downward
8. When he is fully laying down, with elbows, bottom and stomach on the floor, click to tell him he has done the desired behavior
9. Reward with the treat immediately after the click (but not simultaneously!)
10. Allow your dog to stand again by standing up and brining out a treat.
11. Repeat this many times in a row for 3 to 5 minutes and then take a break.
12. Repeat with another training session if your dog is still interested and doing well with the 'down' training session
13. When your dog has mastered this training technique, the next step is saying the 'down' command but just using your empty hand to guide him instead of a treat. Still click and reward with a treat when he has done the desired behavior.
14. The next step is just having your dog respond to the verbal command. Reward with a click and treat
15. When your dog has mastered the 'down' command, begin training in other environments, so your dog does not think he only needs to obey the 'down' command in one room. Slowly move to more challenging environments, leaving outdoors for last.
16. It can take weeks for a dog to master down, so be patient.
17. Stop each training session before you lose your dog's attention. He should go into each training session excited, not worn out from the one that came before. You do not want your dog to start associating training with something boring or painful.

EXTRA TIPS FOR TRAINING 'DOWN'

•   It is common for a dog to pop up to a standing position from the sitting position as you lower the treat to the floor. If your dog does this, make sure not to reward this behavior but to move the treat away, stand up, and start over from the 'sit' command.

•   A trick to get your dog to understand he needs to lay down is to sit with your knees bent in front of you, forming a pyramid or tent shape. You will have your dog on one side of your knees, and the treat on the other, so he basically has to crawl through your legs to get to it. This will force him into the 'down' position.

- If your dog is having trouble learning down, you can reward him any time you spot him lying down around the house. Just surprise him with 'down,' a click and a treat. He will come to associate the command with the position.

- You can use slight pressure on your dog's shoulders to help him get into a laying position, but this is even less effective than using pressure to get him into the 'sit' position, as it is more confusing what you want him to do. Remember never to push or force your dog physically, as this can be painful or scary for your dog.

- Remember to use petting and verbal praise ("good dog!") as well as treats to keep building your relationship with your dog and keep him interested in training.

- As with all dog training, patience is key! Some dogs will learn faster than others.

That is how you teach your puppy to lie down and obey the 'down' command.

In the next chapter, we will learn how to teach your puppy the 'stay' command. Make sure not to move on until your dog has truly mastered 'sit' and 'down,' as these are essential to know before 'stay.'

CHAPTER 9
TEACHING 'STAY'

"A dog is the only thing that can mend a crack in your broken heart"

—*Judy Desmond*

In this chapter, we will learn how to teach your puppy 'stay.' This one can be a bit harder for your dog to learn, as his natural instinct will be to follow you and be close to you, so this trick can be working against his natural instincts.

However, if you have successfully mastered the training of 'sit' and 'down,' (which are necessary to be able to learn 'stay'), then your dog should already be accustomed to "learning how to learn" and he will be excited to master another trick for you.

Without further ado, let's teach your puppy 'stay'!

1. Prepare for the trick:
    a. Establish a good training environment (indoors, familiar, calm, free of distraction)
    b. Make sure your dog is a good mood for training (calm, attentive, not hyper or sleepy or hungry)
    c. Have your clicker and a pocket of healthy, small, bite-size and dog-safe treats at the ready
    d. Make sure your own energy and body language are calm, and you feel confident
2. Get your dog's attention with a click and treat reward
    a. He should be facing you

       b.   This alerts him that a training session will begin

3. Take out a treat from your pocket so that your dog knows you have it
4. Get your dog into the sitting position with the 'sit' command
5. While standing in front of your dog, place your hand, palm facing him, and say the command 'stay.'
   a. Say the command in a happy tone and repeat it several times, but not too many.
6. Take one step back and keep your hand out, and say 'stay' again.
7. If your dog has remained still, give a click and reward treat and praise.
   a. For this step, it is important that the dog not come to you, but that you bring the treat to your dog. Otherwise he will associate getting up and coming to you with getting the reward, and will begin to think that you are training him to get up and come to you. This is the opposite of what we want!
8. If your dog has moved to follow you instead of doing 'stay,' which most dogs will do as they are learning to stay, begin the trick over again with 'sit.'
9. Repeat steps 4 to 8, each time taking one more step back. If your dog is beginning to get up, go back to the step before. (i.e., if your dog keeps getting up after three steps, keeping repeating just taking three steps back until he has a firm grasp on that distance before moving onto four steps back).
10. As your dog gets more comfortable with this trick, begin having him come to you to get the treat. Use the command 'come' but it is not important that he be using the cue of come, just that you use the tone of training that you say your training words in.
11. Stop each training session before you lose your dog's attention. He should go into each training session excited, not worn out from the one that came before. You do not want your dog to start associating training with something boring or painful.

EXTRA TIPS FOR TRAINING 'STAY'

- Remember that short training sessions daily and consistently are much more effective than batching your training. For example, it is better to train for 5 to 10 minutes every day than train for an hour on the weekend.

- Learning 'stay' can be a new kind of behavior for your dog to

SHANNON O'BOURNE & PETER WHITMAN

understand. So far, he has learned 'sit' and 'down,' which are *actions he takes*. 'Stay' is *continuing* or *holding* an action, so it may not be obvious at first.

- Patience, patience, patience, as always

- Train in a comfortable place, not on hard and cold tile or hardwood floors. These can be distracting for your dog if they make him uncomfortable.

- To increase the difficult of the 'stay' command, practice using these additional training techniques:

  o Change environments for added difficulty for your dog during 'stay'
  o Walk away from your dog with your back facing to him
  o Increase the length of time to more than your dog is used to during 'stay'
  o Distract your dog while he stays, like having someone else come into the room, or jumping up and down
  o Go completely out of sight while your dog stays, i.e. behind a wall

That is how to train your puppy to stay! Congratulations, you have officially taught your dog three of the essential commands. Has it been hard work? Do you feel more connected with your dog? Is your dog better behaved? We hope the answer to all three is yes!

And are you ready for more? Get ready to teach the final two essential commands to your dog. Training should be getting easier as your puppy becomes familiar with training sessions.

Remember to practice patience, and that building trust and communication with your dog is the most important part of training.

Let's go on to the next trick, which is the 'come' command, one we've already been introduced to during 'stay' training.

CHAPTER 10
TEACHING 'COME'

"The better I get to know men, the more I find myself loving dogs."

—Charles de Gaulle

In this chapter, you will learn how to teach your puppy to 'come.' We already got a preview of the method for 'come' as you taught your dog 'stay' in the last chapter.

This will be one of the most important behaviors you teach your dog, as it can help you in dangerous or unsafe situations. If your dog escapes out your door or from your yard, being able to train your dog to 'come' back before entering a dangerous roadway or getting into trouble could save his or her life.

As always, this trick will require patience, positive reinforcement, and a good training environment for your dog. For this training method, you will also need a leash.

Let's teach your puppy to 'come'!

1. Prepare for the trick:
    a. Establish a good training environment (indoors, familiar, calm, free of distraction)
    b. Make sure your dog is a good mood for training (calm, attentive, not hyper or sleepy or hungry)
    c. Have your clicker, a leash and a pocket of healthy, small, bite-size and dog-safe treats at the ready

      d.   Make sure your own energy and body language are calm, and you feel confident

2. Leash your dog and stand about six feet away from your dog, or the length of the leash
3. If your dog does not stay still, use the 'sit,' 'down,' and 'stay' commands
4. Walk backward rapidly from your dog while saying 'come'
      a.   Your dog will naturally want to follow you
5. If your dog begins coming toward you, use a click and give a treat reward
6. If your dog does not come toward you, tug on the leash a little bit so that it urges him to get up and begin moving toward you
7. Repeat steps 2 to 6 until your dog understands the command for moving toward you
8. Now you must teach your dog that 'come' means reaching you, not just moving forward several feet. So once you say 'come,' keep moving backward away from your dog, and do not click and reward him until he reaches you.
9. Keep repeating these steps until your dog is comfortable with 'come'
10. Remember to end training sessions before either you or your dog becomes bored or frustrated! If training is going well, you can stop when in a good place, so you can start on a positive note again the next day.

EXTRA TIPS FOR TRAINING 'COME'

- To increase the difficulty and reinforce the 'come' command, do the trick in different locations, with longer leashes, or disappearing entirely from your dog into another room before saying 'come.'

- Be patient with your dog, as all dogs learn at different speeds.

- Try using the 'come' command when you are standing in front of your dog, without moving backward. He should associate the command with coming to you, not just following your lead when you are moving backward from him.

- Train off the leash with your dog in a safe, enclosed area like a back yard.

- Don't increase the distance from your dog, or move off-leash, until your dog is ready and has a firm grasp of the command at the previous distance. It is better to make sure your dog fully understands the command and learns it slowly than moving too quickly and making a mess of the trick.

That is how to teach your dog to 'come'! A puppy that is well-trained in the 'come' command could end up saving his own life by following your call someday, in case he escapes or gets into a dangerous situation.

You have taken action to protect your dog, well done.

In the next chapter, we'll learn the fifth and final essential command that every puppy should know, the 'heel' command, to make your walks more enjoyable.

CHAPTER 11
TEACHING 'HEEL'

"Money can buy you a fine dog, but only love can make him wag his tail."

—Kinky Friedman

In this final trick chapter, you will learn how to teach your puppy to 'heel.' Heeling means that your dog walks alongside you and matches your pace, instead of wandering off on his own and tugging at the leash, or getting distracted.

Some trainers will advocate for use of a 'choke' chain to teach your dog to heal, but using any sort of negative reinforcement against your dog while training him will only cause him to fear you, degrade your trust, and negatively impact your training and relationship overall.

'Heel' is most often used when taking your dog for a walk, and it is essential because, just like 'come', you don't know what can happen in an unpredictable world while going for a walk in public. Perhaps your dog will find something to eat that he should not, or will meet another dog. If you want your dog to stay close to you and pay attention to you, and not pay attention to harmful scraps or a potentially threatening dog, you need to use 'heel.'

Though the goal is ultimately to take your dog outside, we'll still start training in the calm, quiet, indoor environment you have chosen.

So let's teach your dog the fifth and final basic command, 'heel'!

1. Prepare for the trick:

    a. Establish a good training environment (indoors, familiar, calm, free of distraction)

    b. Make sure your dog is a good mood for training (calm, attentive, not hyper or sleepy or hungry)

    c. Have your clicker, a leash and a pocket of healthy, small, bite-size and dog-safe treats at the ready

    d. Make sure your own energy and body language are calm, and you feel confident

2. Have your dog stand next to you on either side, leashed. Choose whichever side feels best to you, and try to always walk with your dog on that side of you.

3. Keep the leash short but with a little lag in it. You will train your dog to come right next to you, with his head by your thigh.

4. Use the 'sit' and 'stay' command, clicking and rewarding for each one to get your dog in position sitting next to you.

5. Now prepare to walk forward with your dog next to you. Take a treat out of your pocket and hold it in front of your dog's nose.

6. Take one step forward, and guide your dog in the correct position with the treat, moving it forward at the same pace, so your dog walks forward. Say the 'heel' command, click and reward.

7. Take another step, repeating the same process of saying 'heel,' and doing a click and giving a reward.

8. Slowly remove the guided treat, and instead take it step-by-step while using your command, clicking and rewarding.

9. Slowly introduce more challenging environments, like going outside.

10. Only when you are ready should you take your dog on an actual walk in public to practice the command.

EXTRA TIPS FOR TRAINING 'HEEL'

• Practice walking your dog enough that he will naturally begin to lag behind you or walk ahead of you. Get him to respond to the 'heel' command in these situations in your back yard or home before going on a proper walk.

• Remember to be patient. 'Heel' is a tough one to learn, as dogs are naturally curious and easily distracted.

That was how to teach your puppy the five essential commands, as well as crate training and potty training. Now your puppy has graduated to the level of a good dog! Feel free to give them extra belly rubs, pets, praise and treats now that you have a graduate on your hands.

Hopefully you have mastered all five of these commands and crate and potty training. If not, do not worry. Training a dog takes a lot of patience, which can be hard for even the calmest person to achieve.

Remember to take frequent breaks, for a mental rest for both you and your dog. Also remember that training should take place over a few days, in short bursts, and not in a long training session once a week.

Even the most rambunctious puppies can be taught these essential commands with patience and understanding.

You've gone a long way towards building the respect and trust of your dog, congratulations! We hope you've learned a lot and had some fun in the process.

CONCLUSION

Thanks again for taking the time to read "Raising the Perfect Puppy."

We love to get real reader feedback, both on what you loved and what we could improve upon. Please write us a short review on Amazon, as it helps us to better serve our readers, and keep producing quality books.

You can leave a review directly at **bitly.com/perfectpuppyreview**

Thank you!

FURTHER READING

If you enjoyed "Raising the Perfect Puppy," you may be ready to move your puppy into more advanced trick training.

Learn how to teach your dog to balance items on his nose, play dead and much, much more:

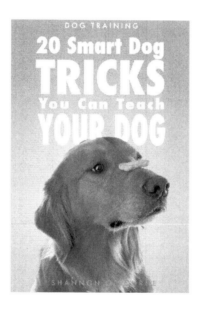

"20 Smart Dog Tricks You Can Teach Your Dog" by Shannon O'Bourne

available in Ebook ($0.99) and Paperback ($5.49) on Amazon at:

bitly.com/20dogtricks

20067582R00034

Printed in Poland
by Amazon Fulfillment
Poland Sp. z o.o., Wrocław